Emotional Intelligence

The Definitive Guide to Understanding Your Emotions, How to Improve Your EQ and Your Relationships

Table of Contents

Chapter 1

Introduction to Emotional Intelligence

There's no escaping the concept of emotional intelligence in today's age. It has suddenly gained a massive momentum everywhere from large corporations to relationship counseling to schools and government agencies. Emotional intelligence is the new psychological health buzzword, and with good reason. It defines your emotional health and interpersonal skills, which are so vital for everyday existence.

The popular phrase was first coined by researchers Peter Salavoy and John Mayer. However, it became popular only in 1996 when researcher-psychologist Dan Goleman published a book titled, *Emotional Intelligence.* So what exactly is the concept of emotional intelligence and why is it such a clinching factor when it comes to choosing people for crucial roles and leading fulfilling personal relationships? Why is everyone feverishly looking for people with a high emotional quotient?

Emotional intelligence as described by Yale psychologist Peter Salovey and John Mayer from the University of New Hampshire is an understanding of one's emotions, empathy for other's feelings and "regulation of emotion in a manner that enhances living." This concept was shortened to make the theory more chewable and interesting for lay people by

Introduction to Emotional Intelligence

Harvard psychologist and New York Times writer Daniel Goleman. His book *Emotional Intelligence* complied years of behavioral research on processing feelings. He broadened the definition of smartness, and sought to establish that brainpower, which is measured by standardized IQ tests may not matter as much as mental qualities when it came to predicting a person's overall life success.

Goleman focused on the practical applications and how organizations can use this information to hire the right candidates, how couples could increase their chances of enjoying lasting relationships, how parents could help raise better children and how educational institutions could teach children more effectively.

Emotional Intelligence is the power to be aware of and recognize your emotions. It is the ability to correctly decipher your emotions and the impact they have on others around you. It is also about how you perceive the emotions of those around you and a high understanding about their feelings, which allows you to be a part of more fulfilling relationships.

In his path breaking book, Daniel Goleman focused on five predominant elements within the emotional intelligence framework, including self awareness, self regulation, motivation, empathy and social skills. Thus, emotional intelligence is an evolved understanding/awareness of not just your emotions but also those of others around you to manage relationships more effectively. No surprise then that emotional intelligence has overtaken other attributes such as skills, knowledge, and intelligence quotient when it comes to job recruitments. Everyone wants people with greater understanding, empathy and social skills to forge stronger relationships.

According to Daniel Goleman's blog, the concept of EQ or Emotional Quotient as a phrase is recognized in diverse languages including, German, Korean, Portuguese and Chinese. There's also a mention of religious scholars from diverse faiths communicating with the author to reinforce how the concept of emotional intelligence or emotional quotient echoes their faith's teachings. Hence, emotional intelligence can be all encompassing. It can be applied to various spheres of your life to gain more physical, mental and spiritual nourishment.

While conventional IQ attempts to evaluate a person's capacity to learn information, EQ is about a person's ability to deal with others effectively. Emotional quotient focused on evaluating soft skills such as managing relationships, showing empathy, self-awareness and social awareness. The human brain is understandably complex and it is impossible to asses a person's success quotient based on a single type of intelligence. Therefore, while IQ evaluates your technical prowess within the field of work, EQ helps you with greater emotional awareness of yourself and others.

There is absolutely no correlation between your IQ and EQ score. Some people possess an excellent academic aptitude yet struggle with handling their and other people's emotions. Haven't we all seen folks who are incredibly brainy, yet are clueless when it comes to dealing with people. IQ and EQ evaluate different types of human intelligence. While the former attempts to measure your cognitive prowess, the latter measures your emotional awareness.

Have you been so overtaken by your emotions that you regretted something you said or did later? Few people can deny this. The fact of the matter is, all of us need emotional intelligence in our everyday lives. We can all benefit from learning to manage our emotions more productively. Emotional quotient helps you forge deeper connections with friends and work associates. It leads to higher interpersonal relationship satisfaction, work performance and the ability to control stressful situations.

A heightened emotional quotient gives you the ability to identify and regulate not just your emotions but also those of others. You have no trouble empathizing with people and being aware of their responses. Emotional quotient awards you the power to manage relationships more productively, even in stressful and conflict laden situations.

Let us take an example to illustrate the concept of emotional intelligence. Ron and Bob both had a big fight with their supervisor at work. Ron didn't possess high emotional intelligence, while Bob was emotionally intelligent. On getting home, Ron began cursing and yelling at his kids who were playing noisily in the house. He acted without thinking about the impact his behavior would have on the kids.

On the other hand, when Bob returned home, he noticed his children playing nosily but told himself that they were simply being kids and doing what they do every day. They were not responsible for his problems with his supervisor or how he was feeling at the moment. Why should they be at the receiving end of his feelings when they have nothing to do with it? This is how Bob rationalizes and maintains his calm.

Did you spot the differences in approach in both these instances? Emotionally intelligent people identify their emotions, give it a good thought before reacting and behave in a more emotionally matured manner. They tend to process their emotions mentally before reacting in haste, and regretting it later, which is a typical sign of low emotional intelligence. People with low emotional intelligence react first and think about their reactions later, while people with higher emotional intelligence think before reacting.

Let us see how emotional intelligence can be practiced in some scenarios we are often confronted with. For instance, your best friend asks you for your opinion about his/her new romantic partner whom you thoroughly disapprove. He/she is extremely excited about his/her newest date, who they claim is the best thing to have ever happened to them. While they believe it's a match made in heaven, you believe it's the ultimate highway to hell. You'd obviously like to help your best friend, but you'd also like to communicate in a manner that doesn't sour things between the two of you. How do you handle the situation?

People with a high emotional quotient will start by objectively evaluating why they dislike their best friend's romantic interest. Are you plain jealous? Does their romantic relationship pose a threat to your relationship with your friend? Does their date remind you of someone whom you have had a terrible experience with? Are you brining your own experiences while evaluating their relationship?

If it is none of this and you are truly convinced that the person is just not good for your friend, you will pose more neutral questions to your friend, which will allow him/her to reflect on the answers on their own rather than go through the agony of hearing their best friend rip apart their romantic interest. If you are emotionally intelligent, you will have a few questions ready to help your friend gather the answers on their own to conclude that the journey with this person may not be as smooth as they are imagining. The idea is to help them realize things on their own without judging, criticizing and making hateful accusations. Also, as someone possessing high emotional intelligence, you must be prepared for being proved wrong.

Let us take another scenario. You have a colleague who you otherwise share a great equation with. She/he is warm, affable and pitches in whenever you require help. However, the problem here is their plainly annoying and overpowering signature perfume. The colleague's sensory receptors seem to be absent and he/she absolutely overdoes the perfume, so much that the suffocating smell makes you sick. You want to voice your objections, yet are wary of offending them because they are genuinely nice. What do you do to make the situation less awkward?

If you are an emotionally intelligent person, you will refrain from offending the other person by being too forthright and assign the blame to your allergies in a more non-confronting and less hurtful manner. Rather than blaming him/her for their tacky fragrance choices that want to make you throw up, you diplomatically assign the onus of blame on your allergies and sensitivities. "I really wish I didn't have such a fine tuned sensory perception." See what we did there? Instead of accusing the other person, you communicated your own allergy or the fact that you and not they are to be blamed for the overpowering smell.

In his bestselling book, "Emotional Intelligence – Why It Can Matter More Than IQ", researcher psychologist Daniel Goleman mentions five crucial elements that define the concept of emotional intelligence.

Self Awareness – People with high emotional intelligence are generally more self aware. They possess a solid understanding of their emotions, the impact of others behavior on their emotions and how their own behavior can affect others. They understand their emotions well enough to not let it rule them. This self awareness makes them more confident, self assured and in control. They rely on their intuition and don't allow emotions to get the better of them.

Self aware people are able to objectively analyze themselves. They are well aware of their strengths and weakness, and use them effectively to achieve the desired results in their personal and professional life. They know what aspects of themselves they need to work on. They seldom live in denial mode. Self awareness is one of the most important aspects of emotional intelligence.

There are several ways to practice self awareness such as meditation, journaling and reflection. For instance, take common stressful scenarios you cope with at work each day such as a team member failing to complete a project on time or being inundated with mails or preparing for an important last minute presentation. What are the emotions these situations elicit in you? Write down your feelings when you are in a more objective mind frame. Include personal stress inducing scenarios too such as being betrayed by a loved one or a breakdown in communication patterns. When you write objectively, it gives you a good insight of your deepest emotions.

Self Regulation – Self regulation is a person's ability to manage or control his/her emotions. Self regulators of feelings and emotions do not allow their emotions to sway them into hasty actions or words. They are seldom angry, impulsive or jealous. Their decisions are well thought out. These are the folks that actually think before acting. People with high emotional self regulation are thoughtful, secure, honest and self-assured. They act with integrity and have little trouble saying no to people where required.

Motivation – People with a high emotional quotient are always raring to go. They are firmly fixated on their goals and motivated to fulfill them. They seldom seek immediate gratification and are willing to give up short term pleasures for long term rewards. Emotionally intelligent people are more solution oriented, productive, challenge embracing and generally efficient in things they take on. Since they operate with a more positive and possibilities mind frame, they are able to stay motivated and chase their goals to fruition.

Empathy – Empathy is the crux of emotional intelligence. It is the ability to recognize and feel the emotions of others from their viewpoint. People with a high empathy quotient are brilliant at indentifying others feelings and emotions, even when they aren't very conspicuous. People with high empathy excel at relationship management, listening, and relating to the troubles of others. This makes them wonderful negotiators and leaders. They rarely judge people quickly and their lives are open books.

Social Skills – People with high social skills are effortless to deal with, which is another vital sign of emotional intelligence. They possess powerful social skills and are generally team players. Instead of obsessing over their own success, they believe in helping everyone around them shine and grow. They are very competent when it comes to managing disputes, communicating with people and building lasting relationships. Unlike folks with low emotional intelligence they do not believe in pulling down others to grow or rise in life.

Emotionally intelligent people focus on creating a win-win situation for everyone involved. They are master motivators and communicators. With their knack for handling people, these guys are the most sought after conflict resolvers and negotiators. Little wonder then than emotional intelligence is one of the most preferred attribute at the senior management level.

Social is skills is tantamount for success in every sphere of personal and professional life. In today's well-connected world, people have quick access to technical information. This is exactly why people's skills is even more crucial than technical skills. There is a greater need to be able to negotiate, identify and empathize with people in a worldwide economy. Businesses need people who can wield influence and use effective persuasion techniques by recognizing other's emotions. There is a need to communicate more clearly, and inspiring groups of people.

Organizations need competent change catalysts that can initiate or manage change efficiently. A social skill also involves conflict management, including negotiation skills and resolving differences. Collaboration, teamwork, cooperation and achieving shared goals become simpler when people possess a high emotional quotient. Pursuing collective objectives and building group synergy is effortless for people with well developed social skills and emotional intelligence.

Emotional Intelligence is a greater awareness of your own feelings, emotions and actions, and how they affect people around you. It is also about valuing others, listening to their needs and being able to empathize/identify with these folks on multiple levels. It is about feeling things from their perspective and reacting in a more appropriate and positive manner.

We all know that one person (or more than one person) in our work or personal life, who is an exceptionally good listener. Irrespective of the situation, they always say the right thing. It's almost like they instinctively know what to say. These people know how to say things to make them less offensive for people. They are caring, empathetic and considerate. Emotional intelligent folks may not necessarily have a solution to all your problems but they possess the ability to leave you feeling more positive and hopeful about the grimmest situation.

By now you've probably figured out that emotional quotient can be one of keys to success, especially in your career and interpersonal relationships. The ability to deal with people's emotions and building relationships is the essence of being a leader. Sharpening your emotional quotient can be a great way to bring out your leadership skills. The best part of emotional intelligence is that it can be developed. Even if you don't possess a very high emotional quotient, there's no reason for you to not work on it consciously and sharpen it.

While some people have an inherent gift of harnessing their emotions and weaving them seamlessly into areas such as problem solving, others keenly work on their EQ to forge more rewarding interpersonal and work relationships. They consciously develop a knack of managing and regulating their own emotions, while sharpening their ability to react to other people's emotions.

Little Cynthia watches her mommy finish a call. "Mommy, what makes you cry?" she inquires. "I am alright Cynthia, I will be ok." Cynthia runs to her room and comes back seconds later. "When I feel sad, I hold Candy in my arms", she said, handing her mother her favorite teddy bear. Cynthia knows her mother's sadness but doesn't believe in crippling her even further.

This is how emotional intelligence works. You understand a person's emotions and you don't make it more devastating for them. There is an attempt to comfort them by sharing the best you can. You don't have to judge, sermonize or lecture people. All they need is to feel secure, safe and comforted.

These guys are pros at managing their feelings. They aren't easily offended or angered even in the most stress inducing circumstances. They look at challenging situations more calmly and are more solution oriented. Emotionally intelligent folks are highly tuned in to their intuition for making important decisions. They have the ability to evaluate themselves more objectively by handling criticism rather well and knowing their areas of improvement.

When we develop the gift of better managing people's emotions and empathizing with their unique perspective, conflict resolution becomes easier. You become a better leader, negotiator, mentor, friend and other roles by being aware of the most compelling needs and desires of others. When you know the fundamental emotions that drive, it is easy to manage to manage your behavior to create a win-win situation. It becomes simpler to give people exactly what they are looking for if you are able to intuitively perceive their needs.

Jason was a highly accomplished and successful manager well-known for his knack of handling challenging organization issues and getting impressive results. He assessed situations accurately, made solid decisions, and took ownership of company projects. Jason swiftly rose from the role of a divisional manager to a senior management position within the firm.

He continued to lobby for senior organizational leadership positions and proactively sought an increase in his functional responsibilities by taking on more challenging problems. He rose to the senior management rank quickly.

Introduction to Emotional Intelligence

Jason was confident, and others believed he would inevitably reach the echelons of management success. He did not end up in the senior executive suite. In fact, his career went downhill and the management had to look for substitutes to reassign his responsibilities. What do you think went wrong with this rather promising manager? Why did his journey to the top go off the course?

This is the story of most senior managers. While they are able to manage people at the junior management level, micromanaging managers and delegating independent authority at the senior level becomes tough. Jason was capable of getting through his behavior at the lower management level. However, once the organization became too large for his control, it was impossible to manage an efficient working relationship with senior managers.

Jason's inability to delegate authority and obsession for micromanagement were indicators of a much larger issue – he simply lacked emotional intelligence. This illustration explains why senior managers need huge reserves of emotional intelligence. Jason struggled with understanding and managing his emotions. This self awareness deficit translated into being unable to comprehend and manage other's emotions.

Jason's greatest handicap was his insecurity and fear. He feared about losing control over his organizational domain if he ceased to micromanage each aspect. His fear of being replaced if his team did their jobs only too well or being unable to control his managers if he gave them complete authority led to his dwindling fortunes. Jason became a victim of his own inability to manage his and the team's emotions.

When negative emotions are unmanageable, organizations are prone to produce disastrous results. It can result in stunted productivity, strained relationships, unmet business objectives and higher absenteeism.

According to a study, surgeons involved in malpractice suits had lesser chances of being sued if they spent an extra 3 minutes doing the following – making orienting statements, using reassuring words and communicating empathy.

Let's do a short self evaluation here to gauge your Emotional Quotient.

1. Are you able to identify your own emotions?

2. Do you quickly register the emotions of other people or are able to understand how they are feeling?

3. Can you point out exactly what triggers emotions within you?

4. Can you control or organize your emotional informational?

5. Are you willing to admit to and learn from mistakes easily?

6. Are you able to control your emotions?

7. Can you listen more than you talk or at least as equivalent to how much you talk?

8. Can you handle criticism positively?

9. Are you calm and composed under the most intense pressure situations?

These questions will help you reflect where you stand in the emotional quotient meter. However, fret not if you do not consider yourself an emotional intelligence superstar. There are tons of ways to boost your EQ.

Chapter 2:

Difference between Intelligence Quotient and Emotional Quotient

How does emotional quotient differ from intelligence quotient? The simple answer is- they measure different forms of intelligence. Your technical acumen or technical skills is a direct result of a high intelligence quotient. You've mastered your skills well, which is a reflection of well-developed cognitive abilities. However, is intelligent quotient enough to determine your success when it comes to dealing with people (unless you are cooped up on a remote island all yourself, you have to deal with people)?

While intelligence quotient measures your technical expertise, emotional quotient evaluates your ability to manage your and other people's emotions in your work and personal life. You know where every employee stands when it comes to technical prowess but do you really understand their thoughts, actions and feelings to be able to better manage your and their behavior in sync with these emotions. When we gain insights into the underlying emotional patterns of people, it becomes easier to relate to them and channelize more productive behavior. This is a fundamental difference between intelligence quotient and emotional quotient.

Difference between Intelligence Quotient and Emotional Quotient

Ever wondered why some of the cleverest people hit a blank in their professional lives and just can't seem to climb the corporate ladder, while the less knowledgeable and inexperienced folks smoothly sail their way to professional success? We all know of people who don't exactly possess the slickest technical skills yet surprisingly manage to reach top management positions. What is it that sets them apart from their more technically competent peers? Emotional intelligence is the key. It is their ability to recognize and control their and other's emotions to build more productive relationships that helps them score.

A person's intelligence quotient demonstrates their core technical competencies, cognitive development and unusual abilities, their emotional intelligence determines their ability to identify emotions and deal with others. Your emotional quotient determines how you will deal with stress, difficult people, bullying, high pressure work situations, conflict within the team, and differences in relationships.

Intelligence is an indicator of your cognitive prowess such as logical thinking, analytical reasoning, memorizing information, solving problems, verbal abilities, creative thinking and much more. Emotional intelligence is controlling your and other's emotions for creating optimally positive circumstances. Starkly different from your ability to comprehend words and numbers, emotional quotient helps you develop healthy interpersonal relationships in your personal and work life.

Emotional intelligence can include stress management, intuition, emotional flexibility, empathy, honestly and more. Emotional quotient highlights your and others emotions with respect to changing circumstances and people, while intelligence quotient is all about cognitive abilities.

While intelligence quotient can determine your success during your academic stint, emotional quotient is vital for all round success in life. You may excel as a student if you possess a high intelligence quotient. However to attain overall success in life, you need a high emotional quotient.

Research has indicated that there are five fundamental skills that distinguish the star performers from low performers. These skills are empathy, self-awareness, assertiveness, problem solving and happiness. Potential recruits who score high on these five attributes are 2.7 times likelier to succeed than folks who bag low scores.

So, why is emotional quotient so closely associated with a person's chances of becoming successful in life? The answer is – awareness of emotions and ability to express themselves confidently. Emotionally intelligent people are experts in gauging people's emotions and altering their pitches/presentations accordingly. Little wonder then that emotionally intelligence is so vital for people in sales, customer service, counseling and other industries.

For instance, a study closely followed the recruitment of sales personnel for cosmetic giant L'Oreal based on their emotional skills. It was observed that these emotionally competent sales people outdid other salespersons by a whopping $91,370 to amass a net revenue growth of $ 2,558, 360. In another research, a national insurance firm discovered that salespersons who were low on emotional skills like initiative, confidence and empathy sold far less policies (average premium of $54,000) that agents who scored high on emotional skills (average premium of $114,000). You get the picture, right? When you show high emotional competencies by being proactive, self confident and empathetic, you are able to connect to potential buyers and help them buy rather than simply sell.

In the workplace, intelligence quotient helps for analyzing, connecting the dots and undertaking research and development. Emotional intelligence is about forging a strong team spirit, leadership, building successful professional relationships, collaboration, service and initiative. Emotional quotient can be gained and enhanced as opposed to intelligence quotient, which is a more inborn and hereditary characteristic.

The goal for businesses isn't to simply hire people who are intellectually competent, but lack emotional or people skills. Today's competitive and social interactions dominated world demands workers who are smart (that's a given), and endowed with more thoughtfulness. The ideal candidate is a combination of emotional intelligence and general intelligence. Since all candidates applying for a position possess more or less the same technical competence, emotional intelligence often becomes a clinching factor when it comes to selecting people for important roles.

Standford-Binet, Woodcock-Johnson Tests of Cognitive abilities and Wechsler are some popular intelligence quotient tests, while Mayer-Salovey-Caruso Test and Daniel Goleman model score test are popular emotional intelligence assessment tests. An Intelligence Quotient test generally involves a collection of standardized questions where participants are assigned precise scores based on their answers. These scores are evaluated with respect to average scores within the age group to establish a person's intellectual capabilities.

Emotional quotient tests, on the other hand, are more challenging to administer because feelings and emotional skills are tougher to depict numerically. While intelligence quotient questions have a definite answer for every question, emotional quotient tests tend to be more subjective and require greater evaluation effort. Unlike IQ tests, there aren't any right or wrong answers. Respondents may not answer questions honestly simply to rank high or may adjust their responses according to what they are currently experiencing, which makes these results more skewed. There may be a tendency on part of the participant to say exactly what the evaluators want to hear rather than responding truthfully.

People possessing a high intelligence quotient are excellent at conducting tasks. They are quick absorbers of new skills and information. However, if they have a low emotional quotient, they tend to overlook their and other's feelings. For instance, when something doesn't turn out according to the way they wanted, these folks tend to lose their temper and lash out at people. While someone who is high on emotional intelligence will learn to control their emotions and get along with people around them. They are extremely effective when it comes to working as a team or working in a leadership role.

The concept of emotional intelligence has gained such a strong momentum that it has impacted a large a large number of areas including the corporate world. Several top organizations have now made emotional intelligence tests mandatory as part of the hiring process, along with intelligence quotient.

Difference between Intelligence Quotient and Emotional
Quotient

In personal relationships, 90 percent of the issues arise due to
lack of emotional intelligence. Everything revolves around
empathy, self awareness, awareness of the other person's
emotions, understanding, communication patterns and the
likes, which are all components of emotional intelligence.

Emotional quotient is not the antithesis of intelligence
quotient. They aren't mutually exclusive. Some folks possess
both in huge quantities, while others possess neither.
Psychologists are keener to explore how the two attributes
balance each other. For instance, how your ability to deal with
stress impacts your ability to focus or learn new information.

Chapter 3:

Benefits of Emotional Intelligence

As discussed earlier, emotional intelligence is our ability to manage our and other's emotions by discriminating among these feelings, and using the information to guide our words, thoughts and actions. To cut a long story short, emotional intelligence is an aggregation of your mental and emotional skills. Emotionally intelligent people enjoy a multitude of benefits in all spheres of life including relationships, career and social life. Here are some ways in which your life can be impacted or benefited if you consciously focus on developing high emotional intelligence.

Stellar Productivity

Emotional intelligence has a high correlation with an individual's work performance. Research has revealed that emotional intelligence is twice as crucial as technical/cognitive abilities even among professions such as engineering. Emotionally intelligent managers, supervisors and leaders are way more effective in managing teams, motivating people and negotiating.

They create a more positive atmosphere with happier workers, who are an asset to any organization. Happier workers translate into higher morale, low absenteeism, reduced attrition rate and higher productivity. This leads to happier customers, more sales and higher profits. Thus emotional intelligence is an invaluable trait when it comes to success at the workplace. Whilst everyone within an organization possesses more or less the same technical competency and educational qualifications, only a few rise up the corporate ladder because of their ability to manage people and their emotions.

An emotionally intelligent leader who understands the true value of identifying and managing emotions can empower his/her subordinates with these skills on a daily basis. Discipline or self regulation is essential when it comes to keeping your emotions in check, avoiding panic, remaining calm and being an asset to the team. Emotionally intelligent folks have little trouble in recognizing and managing potentially destructive emotions that can create stress and lower productivity. The approach is calmer, more confident and efficient. Rather than experiencing a more touchy view, these folks depend on their ability to possess a more realistic view of themselves and others.

Coping With Life Challenges

Don't you sometimes look at some people and wonder how they are able to stay afloat through the most challenging situations and emerge even more successful than before? Chances are, these guys score high on emotional intelligence. Emotionally intelligent folks have the ability to calm their body and mind to view things from a clearer and more objective perspective. Their acts are more mindful and less panic struck.

Greater calmness, objectivity and clarity award you more resilience where life's challenges are concerned. Think about the kungfu fighter who can take on the most powerful opponents by constantly working on martial arts skills. Emotional intelligence equips you with those skills to take on the toughest challenges life throws at you with resilience.

Greater Compassion in Personal and Work Life

One of the best benefits of high emotional intelligence is your ability to demonstrate more compassion for others both in the personal and professional sphere. This compassion allows them to connect with people at much deeper levels to forge meaningful relationships. Compassion can be manifested in several ways, including helping someone dealing with a personal issue by taking on their responsibilities or making small everyday decisions for the comfort/convenience of your employees.

Compassion helps you meaningfully connect with people both in your personal and professional life. You are able to reach out to people efficiently, forge more mutually fulfilling relationships and create an atmosphere of harmony and productivity. Emotional intelligence awards you greater compassion in dealing with people in various personal professional and social scenarios.

Boosted Leadership Skills

Emotionally intelligent folks possess a highly evolved ability in recognizing and understanding factors that drive others, which makes them amazing leaders. They are able to make the most of this invaluable information to strengthen their loyalty and forge stronger relationships with people. A competent leader is intuitively tuned in to the most compelling aspirations and desires of his followers. He knows the "hot buttons" of his employees and exactly how to channelize these "hot buttons" to increase overall productivity and positivity within the work environment.

Emotionally intelligent leaders know how to channelize this information for extracting better performance/productivity from people and keeping them happy. People with a high emotional quotient excel at recognizing the strengths and weaknesses of people and harnessing an individual's virtues for benefiting the team.

High emotional intelligence creates better leaders who are able to inspire greater faith and loyalty by using their team's or follower's or emotional range. They are more aware of their emotions, which allow emotionally intelligent folks to create a harmonious environment. Practicing emotional intelligence makes you a better leader.

Did you know that 67% of all competencies said to be fundamental for high performance in the professional sphere is emotional intelligence? Take the example of the world's most successful CEOs. Amazon's Jeff Bezos passionately talks about getting right into the hearts of his customers in a 2009 YouTube video while announcing the company's Zappos acquisition. When Howard Schultz of Starbucks was a child, his father lost a health insurance claim. This turned him into one of the most empathetic CEOs, who is well known showing his employees thoughtfulness by offering generous healthcare rewards. Little wonder then that these folks are as successful as they are. They understand the emotional pulse of their employees and customers to keep them emotionally gratified.

Emotional intelligence helps in building emotional maturity, boosting social intelligence, preventing relationship problems, enhancing interpersonal communication, helping control emotions, dealing with stress, influencing leadership, helping authorities make sound business change decisions, supporting staff and controlling resistance to change.

Lower Chances of Addiction and Other Emotional Disorders

Addictions are generally a direct result of our inability to cope with emotions. People who struggle to come to terms with their emotions use addiction as a mechanism to avoid the more underlying and deeper prevailing issues. When you fail to recognize and manage negative emotions, there develops an unfortunate pattern of dependency on external factors such as food, nicotine, substance, alcohol, porn and the likes. Addiction is just a means to escape from emotions you aren't willing to deal with.

Emotionally intelligent folks are lesser prone to addiction because of their awareness of their emotions and the ability to manage these emotions. They have a solid understanding of their feelings, and do not struggle to deal with it. Since emotional intelligence makes you happier, more confident and balanced, there is a lesser propensity for dependence on destructive coping mechanisms. They adapt more easily to challenges and changing scenarios in life. Emotionally intelligent people are competent in resolving differences and coming up with more positive solutions. Since they display such a high understanding of their and other's emotions, it becomes easier for them to deal with conflicts.

Emotionally healthy people are less prone to be victims of drug abuse or binge eating disorders, which predominantly originate from much deeper psychological issues.

Boosted Employee Morale and Lower Attrition

Morale may be an intangible concept in the corporate world but its effects are highly measureable. You may not realize the value of a high morale when it's there, but you will definitely know when it's missing. Think about the lateness, early departures, attrition, sick leaves your company suffers from. When leaders take the time to build emotional intelligence and connect with their team members, it reflects in the employee morale.

Emotionally intelligent leaders who build stronger emotional ties with subordinates witness improvement in the team's morale, lower measureable absenteeism, a higher team spirit and a greater desire to contribute to an organization's success. The emotional intelligence skill building cost can be minimal. However, the return on investment can be extremely high.

Let's get real here and call a spade a spade. Employees do not really quit roles, they quit senior managers. It is about escaping people and not positions. Emotionally intelligent leaders, who recognize emotional triggers, quickly pick up emotional clues of their team members and "customize" their approach to each member's unique emotional make-up and motivation will experience greater success in retaining employees. This should not be mistaken with not doing justice to one's own voice or feelings. It simply means, presenting an accurate emotional response towards each team member to treat them with greater compassion, respect and empathy.

The problem with most managers who do not understand the concept of emotional intelligence is that they use a one size fits all approach for dealing with all employees, without understanding the emotional framework, motivators and goals of individual team members. This one size fits all approach does not produce flattering results because personalities vary. Some people are more intrinsically motivated, while others thrive on extrinsic motivation. Some folks are quick to reveal their emotions; others aren't very comfortable sharing their feelings. Once you understand the emotional make-up of people, it becomes easy to deal with them more efficiently.

Fine Communication Skills

People with a well developed emotional quotient are more efficient when it comes to expressing themselves. They possess the ability to listen attentively to other people's verbal clues, while also tuning in to their non verbal communication. They know exactly what to say to channelize people's strengths. They use the right words and non verbal signals to help people feel at ease. There is little scope for misunderstanding whilst communicating with a person who has high emotional intelligence.

Emotionally intelligent people are well aware about the most compelling emotional triggers of the people around them. They know exactly how to inspire people to act. People who are able to communicate by emotionally connecting with are far more effective than technically competent folks who fail to demonstrate empathy while communicating with people. Emotional intelligence awards you better response skills.

Chapter 4:

Proven Tips to Boost Your Emotional Intelligence

After gaining a thorough understanding of emotional intelligence and its benefits, the million dollar question is – is it really possible to improve one's emotional intelligence or emotional quotient? Is it possible from struggling to cope with your and other's emotions to being a rockstar at understanding emotions?

With all its advantages, who wouldn't want high emotional intelligence? Who wouldn't want greater professional success, business potential, leadership skills, relationship gratification, humor, good healthy, positivity and happiness around them? Think about an antidote that beats stress, helps you form rewarding relationships with people and much more.

Take any coaching intervention program, and it will generally highlight some aspect of emotional intelligence in the name of interpersonal skills or social/soft skills. The most compelling reason for this is that, while intelligence quotient is tough to change, emotional quotient can be acquired with training and consistent practice. So, the good news is that even if you do not consider yourself very emotionally evolved, there is plenty of scope to boost your emotional quotient with practice, training and conscious effort.

The best part about enhancing your emotional intelligence is that it can be practiced in your everyday life. For instance, if you are short tempered, start by showing greater empathy or being a more considerate listener.

Emotional Quotient Is Not Rigid

Though our capacity to recognize and handle our and other's emotions is largely determined by childhood experiences, heredity and other factors, it isn't rigid. We can alter our ability to comprehend and manage emotions over the long term with the right coaching and dedication. You can change of course, however, the question is do you want to change? Are you willing to put in the effort required to be more emotionally intelligent? Sometimes, while you may successfully be able to manage your external emotions, you may still grapple with emotions you do not manage to display on the outside.

While some folks are naturally positive, calm and social, others can be plain grumpy, egoistic, shy or insecure. However, no trait is unchangeable. If you truly want to change an aspect of your personality, you can. Emotional intelligence naturally increases with age, without any intervention. This is the rationale behind the popular belief that people gain more maturity as they grow older. Overall, yes it is possible to improve your emotional quotient over the long term with intervention, guidance and regular practice.

Emotional Intelligence Be Developed

Our emotional intelligence pathway originates within the brain going right down to the spinal cord. The primary senses are involved here and must go to the brain's front portion before you start thinking logically or rationally about an occurrence. Emotions are generated in our limbic system, which is why our emotional response to an incident occurs before the rational mind gets involved. Emotional intelligence is based on efficient communication patterns between the brain's logical and emotional points.

Have you heard of plasticity? It is a term used by neurologists for describing the brain's ability to keep evolving and changing. The brain keeps growing newer connections as we acquire new skills. The change is slow, as the brain keeps developing more and more connections to boost its efficiency.

When you use various strategies for boosting emotional intelligence, you are actually letting the microscopic neurons (billions of them) lined between the emotional and logical centers of the brain to branch into smaller arms that touch other cells. This simply means, one cell can form more than 15,000 connections. The chain reaction signifies that it is simpler for the brain to adapt to this new behavior in the long term. Once the brain is trained with the help of emotional intelligence strategies, it becomes a habitual behavior/thought pattern.

Accurate Feedback

One of the most crucial aspects if you want to enhance your emotional quotient through any coaching intervention or self practice program is accurate feedback. People generally do not realize how others perceive them, especially people in senior management positions in organizations.

Though these folks are increasingly motivated, responsible and high on technical skills, they rarely take the time to pause and assess their behavior. In a nutshell, we do not possess a very accurate notion of how nice we come across as. Wishful thinking, misplaced optimism and overconfidence can be factors contributing to this blind spot.

Generally people tend to over evaluate themselves in the niceness department. They believe they are nicer than they actually are. Any effort at increasing your emotional quotient must begin with gaining a thorough understanding your strengths and weaknesses. Use valid and genuine assessment techniques like personality tests or accurate feedback to determine your success with developing a higher emotional quotient.

Some Methods Work More Efficiently Than Others

Some techniques for boosting emotional intelligence such as cognitive behavioral therapy for better psychological flexibility can work better than other methods. Since emotional intelligence is linked to human behavior, it can never be an exact science. The dynamics of human behavior, motivation, communication and feelings will keep changing. You have to identify and evaluate what works for you. While behavioral therapy works wonderfully well for some people, others may find meditation or deep breathing more effective in calming their emotions.

Here are some tried and tested tips for being the ultimate emotional intelligence ninja.

Respond Rather Than React

Reacting is a more unconscious and uncontrolled process that is a result of an emotional trigger. For instance, you snap when someone annoys you or you are already stressed due to another reason.

Responding, on the other hand, is more controlled and something you choose to do. You decide exactly how you behave in the given situation. For example, explaining to someone that you are not feeling too good and that this isn't the best time to interrupt you, and that later you'd be in a much better position to give them a good hearing. You've simply chosen to deal with the situation in a more productive and less impulsive manner by taking control of your emotions.

Evaluate how your actions will impact others before acting. If your behavior will affect others, try and place yourself in their shoes. How are they bound to feel if you say or do something? Would you like to go through the experience yourself? If you have to take a particular action, can you help people in coping with its effects?

Accept Responsibility for Your Feelings and Actions

This can be one of the most challenging yet productive tips for boost your emotional quotient. Your emotions originate from you and therefore you are completely responsible for them.

People around you may be responsible for creating certain situations but it is ultimately you who are in charge of your reaction to those situations. You may not always be able to control how others around you speak or behave. However, the way you react to their words and actions is something you have control over.

If you are hurt by someone and lash out, you are the one responsible for it. Get out of the mindset that "someone makes you do something." No one can make you angry; you are responsible for your anger. No one holds the strings to your emotions. No one makes you do or feel anything. Your reaction is completely your own responsibility. Your feelings can offer you important guidelines about your experience with different people along with your own requirements and preferences. However, your feelings and actions are no one's but your responsibility.

Once you start accepting responsibility for your feelings and behavior, it becomes simpler to manage it for impacting all spheres of your life positively.

If you hurt people, be gracious enough to accept it and apologize. Ignoring the person or not accepting the responsibility for your behavior is not a sign of high emotional intelligence. Your relationships will be much more positive and people will forgive you more easily if you make an honest attempt to set things right rather than live in denial land. Accepting your mistakes, apologizing and moving on is a sign of high emotional intelligence.

Be Assertive

Emotionally intelligent folks know the importance of setting appropriate boundaries to let people know our stand. You have the right to disagree with people without acting in a disagreeable manner. Learn to say refuse without feeling guilty when you are not up to something or you find people taking advantage of you. Set your priorities and safeguard yourself from stress, harm and duress.

Rather than using "you" followed by the accusation and putting people on the defensive foot, try making them more open to listening to and understanding your point. For instance, instead of saying "you should do this" or "you are xyx", try saying, "I feel really uncomfortable when you expect me to do this over my priorities" or "I strongly believe that I deserve recognition from the organization based on my consistent performance and contributions." See what we did there? We aren't putting people on the defensive by pointing a finger at them and saying, "you did this" or "you are like this." We are being assertive and talking about our feelings without blaming anybody.

Pay Close Attention to Your Behavior

You can only manage your emotions more effectively if you are consciously aware of it. It starts with paying very close attention to your emotions and their impact on your behavior. Emotional awareness is one of the cornerstones of EQ.

Start noticing how you act when you experience specific situations, and how it affects your everyday life. Do these feelings impact your productivity? How about your communication with other people? Do your emotions pose a threat to your overall well-being, including your physical and emotional health? How do you react when you are extremely angry, happy or sad? Once you are consciously aware of your reactions to emotions, you will be able to wield better control over them and channelize them more productively.

Practice Empathy

Empathy is all about trying to understand why someone feels or acts in the way they do by putting yourself in their shoes. It is also being able to communicate this understanding to them more effectively. Empathy can also apply to your emotions and feelings.

Each time you notice yourself experiencing a specific emotion or behavior, try and think why you feel the way you do. You may not be able to figure it out at the onset but pay close attention and you'll start receiving various answers that you didn't notice earlier.

When someone is experiencing a rather strong feeling, ask yourself how you would feel in a similar scenario. Always be interested in what people say to respond in a more sensitive manner. It is always a good practice to ask questions and summarize what people say so you are clear, and people know you are actively listening to them.

When you put yourself in the other person's shoe, you reduce reactivity. For instance, if your child is resisting something you are telling him/her, try thinking it isn't easy for them to deal with peer pressure and academics. Think for a moment how it must be to be a young kid in the current competitive age.

If your manager is being demanding and difficult, think about the pressure of performance expectation they are dealing with at the hands of senior management. When you start thinking more objectively by considering where the other person is coming from, understanding and conflict resolution become much simpler.

Managing other's emotions requires maturity, skill and tact. It starts by being aware of exactly where you want the person to go? Do you want to lead them to feeling happier, calmer, more aware, secure, vigilant or cautious, for instance? Once you realize how they are feeling and how to lead them there, you will know what to say and do.

We tend to forget how particular experiences feel; even we've lived through it ourselves. You can only imagine how much perspective limiting it becomes if we've not experienced what the other person is going through. What is the best way to bridge this gap? The nucleus of empathy lies in understanding the "why" among other things. Why does this person feel the way they do? What are they dealing with that I fail to see? Why do I experience different feelings than them? Explore your "whys" and you will be well on your way to better understanding the feelings of others.

Being kind, considerate and helpful is one of the best ways of practicing emotional intelligence.

Avoid Labeling Your Emotions

All your emotions are valid, including the not so positive ones. Avoid assigning labels and judging your emotions. When you judge your feelings, you inhibit your ability to experience them. When you cannot fully express or experience something, you prevent yourself from using these emotions more positively.

Each emotion you experience is a vital piece of information closely linked with what is happening around you and how it affects you. Without information about your emotions, you'd be left clueless about how to react to your emotions and manage them more effectively.

Connect negative feelings to events but avoid judging them to gain a better understanding. For instance, if you feel envious, try and figure out what the emotions is conveying to you about the situation. Learn to experience positive emotions so you recognize each opportunity to feel them to the fullest.

Practice Being More Light Hearted

When you are more light hearted and optimistic, it is simpler to capture the goodness of everyday situations and objects. Positivity results in greater emotional happiness and increased opportunities. People are forever looking to be around optimistic folks who come up with positive connections and possibilities. When you become more negative, you only concentrate on what can go awry rather than building strong resistance.

People with a more evolved emotional quotient know how to utilize wit and humor to make everyone feel happier, positive and safer. They know the art of using laugher to tide over tough times.

Use Your Mental Pause Button

Use your mental pause button each time you find yourself on the verge of speaking or acting. Take a moment, breathe deeply and think before you respond. Whenever you feel tempted to type an elaborate mail in rage, stop and think if it is going to help resolve the issue or only make it worse. Each time you feel like screaming at someone or making a combustible comment on the social media, apply the pause button.

When you consciously work on pausing before you speak or act, you get into the habit of thinking before acting or speaking in a manner that can worsen any situation. You learn to manage, control and tackle your emotions to handle any situation in a more constructive manner. When you learn to use this technique, you realize that the button to your feelings and emotions is in your hands.

When you sense a challenge in controlling impulses, deal with it by quickly diverting your attention. Distract your thoughts by counting or concentrating on a pre-planned diversion thought. Your mind can be trained to shift thoughts or conversations fast.

Practice Active Listening

During arguments or disagreements we often listen not to understand but to react and respond. When the other person is speaking, we are almost mentally constructing out own arguments to answer back or give back to them. This leads to even more conflict.

Dealing with conflict becomes more effective when you tackle issues in an assertive yet respective manner, without being defensive. When you listen empathetically, your own thoughts and emotions are taken into account. Listening actively and empathetically can help you shed toxic feelings building up in you.

Be assertive by all means, but also practice active listening to find that one point that can lead to resolution. Problem solution only happens when you understand where the other person is coming from and what they want. You can find a middle ground only when you tune in to the words, feelings and emotions of the other person, not just to give a fitting reply but also to resolve the issue. Listening is all about putting the other person's words, thoughts and feelings first.

Your opinion about people or events may not change. However, the time spent listening to the other person may just calm you and help you come up with a more positive or constructive response. It may help you see things from a different perspective and analyze the situation more objectively.

Be Open to Feedback

Boost your emotional intelligence by being more receptive to feedback. While you may disagree with the criticism/feedback, sometimes being open to other's views can help you identify behavior patterns that may be having an effect that you didn't intend. Healthy feedback can guard you from blind spots and adjust your behavior.

The more you exist in denial mode about destructive behavior, the more challenging it may be for you to develop a high emotional quotient. Acceptance and awareness is the key to increasing your emotional intelligence.

Practice Deep Breathing

Strong emotions impact us physically too. When we are stressed or anxious, our bodies respond in a more evolutionary instinctive manner like we're face to face with a nature based threat. The physical reactions include constricted blood vessels, shallow breathing and speedier heart rate.

When we learn to consciously manage our body's reaction to anxiety, the emotional attribute is lowered. Each time you feel nervous or tense, practice slow and deep breathing. Concentrate on the flow of the breath and the abdominal cavity. You will invariably feel better and calmer once you relax and create more space in your mind.

Mindfulness or mindful breathing is another way to achieve stillness of the mind by completely immersing yourself in the present non-judgmentally. When you get into the habit of identifying your thoughts and emotions with judgment, you boost your awareness and gain greater clarity rather than operating from a judgmental and assumption laden point of view. Mindfulness reduces your chances of being overtaken by negative or destructive emotions.

Decrease Negative Personalization

When we feel negatively impacted by someone's behavior, do not rush into a conclusion. Tempting as it is to ascribe a negative reason for their behavior, try to gather a more holistic perspective of the circumstances before reacting. For instance, it is easy to think a friend isn't returning your call or message because he/she wants to avoid you.

However, they may also be busy or ill or in a dire situation. When we avoid ascribing negative reasons or personalizing people's behavior, we view them more objectively and with less hateful/judgmental emotions. The ability to overcome negative personalization of people's behavior is critical for boosting your emotional quotient.

Develop Flexibility

Sometimes we get stuck in our own monotonous traps and become rigid and inflexible, which may impair our emotional intelligence. People with a highly developed emotional quotient know when to adapt and keep pace with newer techniques rather than getting stuck in an increasingly unproductive cycle. They know when how to adapt and manage their emotions according to the situation. Emotionally intelligent folks know when to adapt and shift perceptions.

Those who possess a highly developed emotional quotient are always open to newer experiences, challenging opportunities and a variety of adventures. Be open to change and shed the uneasiness and inhibitions attached with change.

Learn to decipher the consequences of your words and behavior. Emotionally intelligent folks pick their battles very selectively. They realize that peace and relationships are more valuable than being right.

When you learn to evaluate the consequences of your words and actions and demonstrate more flexibility and adaptability in your actions/words, you display high emotional intelligence. This isn't to be mistaken with letting people walk all over you. By all means, be assertive. However, know that it's not about being right or winning arguments all the time. Emotional intelligence is being perspective enough to realize what is worth fighting for and what is worth giving up.

Read Body Language

Try to gauge people's innermost emotions by tuning in to their body language. Pick up clues about their emotional health by observing their body language. Sometimes people say something while their expressions and gestures convey the opposite or a deeper truth they aren't comfortable revealing. When you practice being more mindful of their body language, you tap into their true emotional fabric to adapt you responses and reactions. Sometimes people resort to less conspicuous ways for communicating their emotions.

For instance, a person may try saying something reassuring but the high tone of their voice may defeat those words and indicate high stress. These are small yet powerful indicators of people's behavior patterns and reading them correctly will give you the power to unlock other's emotional framework.

Be Emotionally Honest

Be emotionally honest and transparent. You are not communicating genuinely if you shut yourself off from expressing emotions. If you say you are alright with a sorrowful face, you are being dishonest in your communication. When you practice being more real about emotions, it is easier for people to read it. It is always great to be able to be yourself and share your real feelings. It helps people know your feelings and understand where you are coming from. They trust you more, which sets the base for more rewarding relationships.

By all means manage your emotions so as to avoid hurting others but misleading others about your emotions or denying real deeper emotions is not a sign of high emotional intelligence.

Be Positive and Happy

How would you rate your happiness quotient on a scale of 1 to 10? Emotional intelligence originates from being happy and vice versa. They aren't simply happy because good things are happening to them but because they are great at managing and taking control of their own happiness.

Happiness originates from within. A person who is capable of managing his emotions efficiently wakes up joyfully each morning. These people encounter challenges too, just like everyone else. However, they do not let these issues dampen their zest for positivity. Develop greater emotional intelligence by keeping your mind clear, avoid getting caught in destructive self-pity and take charge of your happiness. Emotional intelligence comes with being more positive and solution oriented.

Happy people gain more appreciation and following from people to help them tide over tough times. They spread more happiness, live longer and come up with constructive solution. It is a misconception that happiness is a result of material possessions. Genuinely happy people are those who can manage their emotions well, spread happiness, and most importantly those who focus on giving rather than receiving. Emotionally intelligent people know that it costs zilch to be happy and yet the returns are invaluable.

Stop Complaining

One of the first steps towards boosting your emotional intelligence is to stop complaining. Shed the victim syndrome and know that the solution to your problem is well within your grasp. Emotionally intelligent people rarely blame others or their circumstances for the challenges in their life. Instead, they search for matured ways to dissolve a relationship or talk to people who've wronged them in private. They also have a steady stream of effective coping mechanisms such as yoga, meditation, nature trips or simply venting their feelings by writing.

Listen to Physical Clues

Some of the best indicators of our emotional condition are the physical signals our body gives us. You can develop a greater awareness of your emotions simply by tuning in to your physical sensations. You may feel a knot in your tummy while commuting to work, which can be a sign of high stress.

Similarly, when you are with someone you've recently started dating, and experience a too strong to ignore flutter in your heart, it could be an indication of having found the person who'd like to spend the rest of your life with. Our body is constantly trying to communicate emotions we may not be aware of through physical sensations. Listening to these feelings and emotions signaled by the body helps process our emotions and reactions more efficiently.

Tap Into Your Subconscious Mind

How can you gain a greater awareness of your subconscious emotions or feelings? Apart from deep breathing and mindfulness, let your thoughts wander freely and evaluate where they go. Pay close attention to your dreams. Are there any recurring symbols that can be closely connected with the current events in your life?

Keep a journal and pen next to your bed and write down the details you can recall about your most compelling dreams as soon as you are up. Analyze the emotions and patterns of these dreams, their symbolic references and the message they are trying to communicate. When you gain a thorough understanding of the emotions that dominate your subconscious mind, it becomes simpler to train your subconscious mind to guide your actions.

Sometimes, our conscious minds are unable to come with solutions we are faced with, which is why the phrase "sleep over it" originated. Our subconscious mind's functionality is at its peak when we are asleep. Ever wondered why many a times the solution to our problems strikes us when we are asleep? Or we wake up with a totally different perspective or solution much to our surprise? Our subconscious mind is ticking overtime when our conscious mind is resting. By tuning into our subconscious mind, we are tapping into our inner most emotional reserve to uncover our deepest feelings.

Resolve Conflicts Like a Boss

One of the best tips for developing high emotional quotient is mastering conflict management skills. Conflict resolution actually puts your emotional intelligence to practical use.

Resolving differences and conflicts involves many aspects including identifying feelings, clear expression of thoughts, active listening, staying calm and coming up with a solution that diffuses the situation rather than escalating it. When we struggle to understand and control our feeling, we experience a sense of irritation, depression and erratic behavior patterns. Conflicts only get magnified, making it all the more stressful for to deal with. Once you recognize yours and other's emotions, and learn to manage them, you enjoy a happier and more balanced life.

Conclusion

Thank you for downloading this book.

I hope the book was able to help you to understand the powerful concept of emotional intelligence and how you can use it in your everyday life to enjoy more rewarding personal and professional relationships.

There are lots of real life examples, actionable tips and practical pointers on how you can go about boosting your emotional quotient right away.

The next step is to simply take action and follow the proven techniques mentioned in the book.

Lastly, if you enjoyed reading the book, please take time to share your views with us by posting a review. It'd be highly appreciated!

Here's to your rewarding, enriching and emotionally healthy relationships!

www.ingramcontent.com/pod-product-compliance
Lightning Source LLC
Chambersburg PA
CBHW051012050726
47592CB00007B/2813